Daily Activity Bank

PEARSON

Scott
Foresman

Editorial Offices: Glenview, Illinois • Parsippany, New Jersey • New York, New York
Sales Offices: Parsippany, New Jersey • Duluth, Georgia • Glenview, Illinois • Coppell, Texas • Ontario, California

www.sfsocialstudies.com

Contents

ISBN 0-328-03922-5

3 4 5 6 7 8 9 10 V008 10 09 08 07 06 05 04

Fast Fact 1

The cable cars are unique to the city of San Francisco. Tourists ride them up and down the hills of the city.

In what state and region is the city of San Francisco?

Geography

History

Fast Fact 2

More United States presidents were born in the state of Virginia than in any other state.

Name the presidents who were born in Virginia.

Fast Fact 3

Barbed wire, steel wire with thornlike barbs on it, was invented by Joseph Glidden of DeKalb, Illinois, in 1874.

How did barbed-wire fences change the economy of the West, Southwest, and Midwest?

Economics

Fast Fact 4

Two women were married to presidents of the United States and were also mothers of presidents of the United States.

Who are these women?

Fast Fact 5

Univac, one of the first computers, was introduced in the 1950s. It was as big as a room!

Describe the computer that you use at school or at home.

Culture

Geography

Fast Fact 6

The tallest bridge in the world is in Colorado. The suspension bridge over the Royal Gorge of the Arkansas River is 1,053 feet tall.

In what region is the state of Colorado?

Fast Fact 7

More than 12 million immigrants passed through the immigration center on Ellis Island in New York between 1892 and 1924.

Where did most immigrants from China arrive?

History

Economics

Fast Fact 8

Don Wetzel of the United States invented the automated teller machine, also called an ATM or a cash machine, in 1969.

What is the job of a person who is a bank teller?

Fast Fact 9

In 1967 Thurgood Marshall became the first African American to serve on the Supreme Court of the United States.

To which branch of government does the Supreme Court belong?

Government Citizenship

Culture

Fast Fact 10

Solomon Butcher, a native Nebraskan, was famous for the photographs he took of Midwestern pioneer families.

What building material did many early pioneers in the plains states use to build their homes?

Fast Fact 11

Mt. McKinley in Alaska, the highest peak in the United States, is also called *Denali* by Native Americans. *Denali* means "the High One."

What is the lowest point in the United States?

Geography

History

Fast Fact 12

Independence Day is celebrated on July 4 in the United States. Mexican Independence Day is celebrated on September 16.

From what country did Mexico gain its independence?

Fast Fact 13

Early colonists used tobacco as money.

Who makes the money we use in the United States today?

Economics

Fast Fact 14

Wanted! The FBI began its "Ten Most Wanted Fugitives" list in 1950.

What do the letters FBI stand for?

Fast Fact 15

Many early amusement parks in the United States were built by streetcar companies. They built the parks at the ends of their streetcar lines to attract riders!

What kinds of public transportation are available in your community?

Culture

Geography

Fast Fact 16

Rachel, Nevada, has a highway named the Extraterrestial Highway because so many people have claimed to see UFOs, or unidentified flying objects, nearby.

In what region of the United States is Nevada?

Fast Fact 17

On July 20, 1969, astronaut Neil Armstrong became the first man to set foot on the moon.

What American inventors flew the first airplane?

History

Economics

Fast Fact 18

Florida grows more citrus fruit than any other state.

Why is the climate of Florida good for growing citrus fruit?

Fast Fact 19

Election Day is always the first Tuesday after the first Monday in November.

If this year were an election year, on what date would Election Day fall?

Government Citizenship

Culture

Fast Fact 20

Georgia O'Keeffe was an artist famous for her paintings of flowers and of the New Mexico landscape.

Describe the geography of the state of New Mexico.

Fast Fact 21

In the early 1800s earthquakes near New Madrid, Missouri, were so powerful that they caused the Mississippi River to change course.

Where does the Mississippi River begin and end?

Geography

History

Fast Fact 22

In 1838–1839 thousands of Cherokee Indians died when they were forced by the United States government to relocate to Oklahoma. The route they took is called "The Trail of Tears."

Who invented the written language for the Cherokee?

Fast Fact 23

The Mall of America in Bloomington, Minnesota, is the largest shopping mall in the United States.

Why might shoppers use a budget?

Economics

Fast Fact 24

In Australia citizens of voting age are required to vote in general elections.

At what age is a citizen of the United States first able to vote?

Fast Fact 25

Germany developed the frankfurter and Vienna developed the wiener. Americans now eat sausages like these and call them hot dogs.

What foods can you think of that are considered "American"?

Culture

Geography

Fast Fact 26

An estimated one million bathtubs of water pour over Niagara Falls every second.

From what two countries can you view Niagara Falls?

Fast Fact 27

John Glenn, the first man to orbit Earth, returned to space in 1998 at the age of 77, for a space shuttle mission.

In what state and region is the Kennedy Space Center, the place from which the space shuttles are launched?

History

Fast Fact 28

Idaho leads the nation in the production of potatoes.

Are potatoes an import or an export in Idaho?

Fast Fact 29

The job of Congress, the Senate and the House of Representatives, is to pass laws to govern the country.

How many senators are there? How many representatives are there?

Government Citizenship

Culture

Fast Fact 30

February is Black History Month in the United States.

Name a famous African American and explain why that person is celebrated.

Fast Fact 31

Please pass the salt! Utah's Great Salt Lake contains six billion tons of salt.

In what region is the state of Utah?

Geography

History

Fast Fact 32

New York City was the nation's first capital, and Philadelphia was the second.

What is the capital of the United States today?

Fast Fact 33

The back of a dollar bill has thirteen stars and stripes, thirteen olive leaves, and thirteen layers on the pyramid. Why? They represent the thirteen colonies!

Whose picture is on the front of a dollar bill?

Economics

Government Citizenship

Fast Fact 34

Four United States presidents have been assassinated: Abraham Lincoln, James Garfield, William McKinley, and John F. Kennedy.

Who takes over the presidency if the president dies in office?

Fast Fact 35

A new bridge that crosses the Charles River in Boston, the Leonard P. Zakim Bunker Hill Bridge, is ten lanes wide!

What bridges are near where you live? What bodies of water do they cross?

Culture

Geography

Fast Fact 36

The Atlantic Ocean is the world's second largest ocean. And it is getting wider by about one inch a year!

What states border the Atlantic Ocean?

Fast Fact 37

On August 9, 1974, President Richard M. Nixon resigned from office. He is the only president to quit the job.

Who became president after Nixon?

History

Economics

Fast Fact 38

Fifty! That's about how many television commercials an average child in the United States watches each day.

What is the purpose of television commercials?

Fast Fact 39

Delaware became the first state of the United States because it was the first to agree to the Constitution.

What are changes to the Constitution called?

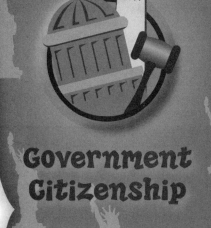

Government Citizenship

Culture

Fast Fact 40

The hula dance is a traditional dance of Hawaii. It is a way of sharing Hawaiian culture.

What traditional dances, songs, or games are part of your culture?

Fast Fact 41

The Pacific Ocean is bigger than all of the continents put together. It covers about one-third of the globe.

What states have borders on the Pacific Ocean?

Geography

History

Fast Fact 42

The first shots of the Civil War were fired at Ft. Sumter in South Carolina.

When did the Civil War begin and end?

Fast Fact 43

Energy companies in California, Pennsylvania, and Oregon are building *wind farms* to create electricity.

Is wind a renewable or nonrenewable resource?

Economics

Government Citizenship

Fast Fact 44

During a presidential inauguration, the president takes an oath. The president promises to lead and protect the country.

What branch of government is the president in charge of?

Fast Fact 45

Pretty corny! Mitchell, South Dakota, is home to the Corn Palace, which is made of corn, of course!

Where else might you visit on a trip to South Dakota?

Culture

Geography

Fast Fact 46

The only rain forest in North America is in the state of Washington.

Explain how to find Washington on a map of the United States.

Fast Fact 47

Since 1791 the Constitution has been amended, or changed, twenty-seven times.

What are the first ten amendments to the Constitution called?

History

Economics

Fast Fact 48

Your money has an identity! Every paper bill has its own serial number.

Where on a paper bill will you find the serial number?

Fast Fact 49

Have you heard of these party animals? The donkey is a symbol of the Democratic Party. The elephant is a symbol of the Republican Party.

Would the current president wear a donkey pin or an elephant pin?

Government Citizenship

Culture

Fast Fact 50

Wow! The Louisville Slugger Museum in Kentucky has a 120-foot baseball bat standing outside of the building!

What equipment do you need to play your favorite sport?

Fast Fact 51

The population of the world is greater than six billion people!

Write the number for six billion. How many zeroes does it have?

Geography

History

Fast Fact 52

More Civil War battles were fought in Virginia than in any other state.

Which eleven states seceded, or left, the Union to form the Confederacy?

Fast Fact 53

China and the United States lead the world in the growing of apples.

Name a state in which apples are a major crop.

Economics

Fast Fact 54

Only nine men who were vice-presidents ran for office and were elected president.

Who are the vice-presidents who were elected president?

Fast Fact 55

Touchdown! The first play-by-play radio broadcast of a football game took place in College Station, Texas, in 1919.

What forms of communication do we depend on today for news and for entertainment?

Culture

Geography

Fast Fact 56

The deepest cave in the United States is in Carlsbad National Historic Park in New Mexico. The cave is almost 2,000 feet deep.

What states border New Mexico?

Fast Fact 57

In 1867 Russia sold Alaska to the United States for about seven million dollars. Alaska became a state in 1959.

What natural resources can be found in Alaska?

History

Economics

Fast Fact 58

The Erie Canal opened in 1825, providing a way for ships to get from the Atlantic Ocean to the Great Lakes.

How does transportation affect the price of goods?

Fast Fact 59

Inauguration Day for the president and vice-president of the United States is always on the January 20 following the election.

How often are a president and a vice-president inaugurated?

Culture

Fast Fact 60

In 1947 Jackie Robinson became the first African American to play Major League baseball. He played for the Brooklyn Dodgers.

Name a famous African American sports figure and tell about his or her accomplishments.

Fast Fact 61

Almost twenty percent of the world's supply of fresh water is in the Great Lakes.

Name the five Great Lakes. In what regions of the country are they found?

Geography

History

Fast Fact 62

In 1803, the United States paid France about 15 million dollars for the Louisiana Purchase. The new land almost doubled the size of the United States.

Describe the area covered by the Louisiana Purchase.

Fast Fact 63

The federal minimum hourly wage was $0.75 per hour in 1950. Fifty years later it was $5.15 per hour.

How are wages and salary alike? How are they different?

Economics

Government Citizenship

Fast Fact 64

The Secret Service is part of the Department of the Treasury.

What important job does the Secret Service perform?

Fast Fact 65

The National Air and Space Museum in Washington, D.C., has Charles Lindbergh's plane, *The Spirit of St. Louis,* in its collection.

What sights would you like to see if you visited Washington, D.C.?

Culture

Geography

Fast Fact 66

The Missouri River is the longest river in the United States. The Mississippi River is the second longest.

What ten states does the Mississippi pass through or by on its way to the Gulf of Mexico?

Fast Fact 67

Texas, which became a state in 1845, is nicknamed the Lone Star State.

What is the nickname of your state?

History

Economics

Fast Fact 68

The bald eagle—which isn't really bald—is on the back of every dollar bill.

Why is the bald eagle shown on the back of dollar bills?

Fast Fact 69

The White House was ready for occupancy on November 1, 1800.

Who was the only president who did not live in the White House?

Government Citizenship

Culture

Fast Fact 70

The winner of the 2000 Indianapolis 500 automobile race, held in Indianapolis, Indiana, was Juan Montoya. He averaged about 167 miles per hour!

Why else is the city of Indianapolis important to the people of Indiana?

Fast Fact 71

Lake Chargogagogmanchaugagog-chaubunagungmaug is in Massachusetts. It is the lake with the longest name in United States.

What states border Massachusetts?

Geography

History

Fast Fact 72

Queen Isabella of Spain was the first woman featured on a United States commemorative coin. It was an 1893 coin.

Why would the United States feature a Spanish queen on one of its coins?

Fast Fact 73

Wall Street is the home of the New York Stock Exchange.

What do you own when you own a share of stock?

Economics

Government Citizenship

Fast Fact 74

The United States Postal Service has designated two-letter abbreviations for states to be used when mailing letters and packages.

What are the abbreviations for the states in the region where you live?

Fast Fact 75

Baseball's first World Series was played in 1903. The Boston Red Sox defeated the Pittsburgh Pirates five games to three.

What is your favorite baseball team? In what city is it located?

Culture

Geography

Fast Fact 76

The state of Illinois has the nickname "The Prairie State."

What is the nickname of your state?

Fast Fact 77

The Seneca Falls Convention in 1848 began the struggle for women's suffrage in the United States.

What is a suffragette?

History

Economics

Fast Fact 78

In 1965 Cesar Chavez organized a grape boycott. He wanted better working conditions for the farm workers who picked the grapes.

How is a boycott different from a strike?

Fast Fact 79

The first capital of the nation of Texas was Houston, named after Sam Houston, the first president of the Republic of Texas.

What is the current capital of the state of Texas?

Government Citizenship

Culture

Fast Fact 80

¿Habla español? **Many people in the state of California speak both Spanish and English.**

What Spanish words can you name that have become part of our English vocabulary?

Fast Fact 81

Hawaii is known as the Aloha State.

What makes Hawaii different from the other forty-nine states?

Geography

History

Fast Fact 82

Suzanna Dickinson and her daughter Angelina survived the bloody battle at the Alamo on March 6, 1836.

Who was fighting whom at the Battle of the Alamo? Who won?

Fast Fact 83

The discovery of oil in Beaumont, Texas, in 1901, was the beginning of the petroleum industry in Texas.

Why is oil sometimes called "black gold"?

Economics

Fast Fact 84

Fourteen state capitol buildings are made of limestone from Indiana.

What is the difference in meaning between the words *capital* and *capitol*?

Fast Fact 85

Cinco de Mayo is celebrated on May 5 in places in the United States with large Mexican American populations.

What does Cinco de Mayo commemorate?

Culture

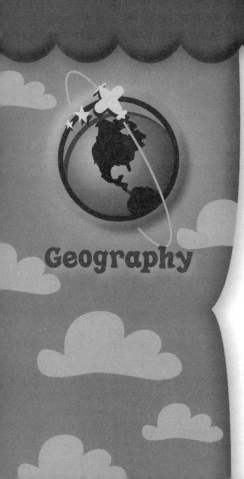

Geography

Fast Fact 86

If you go to Four Corners, you can stand in four states at once! Four Corners is the only place in the United States where four states meet.

What four states meet at Four Corners?

Fast Fact 87

On June 19, 1865, federal troops arrived in Galveston, Texas, to enforce the Emancipation Proclamation. The day is commemorated with a Juneteenth Celebration.

Who wrote the Emancipation Proclamation?

History

Economics

Fast Fact 88

How much? The Duesenberg, a handcrafted luxury car favored by Hollywood stars in the 1920s and 1930s, cost between $15,000 and $20,000, which was extremely expensive back then.

What effect do you think the economy had on the Duesenberg's disappearance from the car market in 1937?

Fast Fact 89

NASA astronauts train at the Lyndon Johnson Space Center in Houston, Texas.

Who was Lyndon Johnson?

Government
Citizenship

Culture

Fast Fact 90

Who knew? Barbecue is an imported idea! The style of cooking was brought to South Carolina by enslaved Haitians.

Find Haiti and South Carolina on a map to trace the origins of barbecue.

Fast Fact 91

The Great Wall of China is so wide that you can ride six horses side by side along its top.

On what continent is the country of China?

Geography

History

Fast Fact 92

Mayas were the first people in the Americas to have a written language.

Where was the Mayan Empire located?

Fast Fact 93

King Henry IV of France wanted to develop a colony of fur traders in North America.

How do you think plentiful supply of beaver pelts from America affected the price of hats made of beaver fur in France?

Economics

Government Citizenship

Fast Fact 94

The flag of the Confederacy during the Civil War was called the "Stars and Bars."

What nicknames are there for the flag of the United States?

Fast Fact 95

The Creeks, Native American people from the Southeast, held a Green Corn Ceremony every year when the corn was ready to be harvested. They gave thanks for a successful crop.

What similar holiday did the Pilgrims celebrate?

Culture

Fast Fact 96

The coastline of Texas stretches more than 600 miles and contains more than 600 historic shipwrecks.

What major body of water does Texas border?

Fast Fact 97

George Washington Carver, a famous African American scientist, made more than 300 products from peanuts and more than 100 products from sweet potatoes.

Name another famous scientist or inventor, and explain that person's contribution to the world.

History

Economics

Fast Fact 98

The King Ranch in the Rio Grande Valley is larger than the state of Rhode Island.

What kind of business is done at the King Ranch?

Fast Fact 99

George W. Bush is the fourth Texan to become President of the United States.

What important state government office did George W. Bush hold before being elected President?

Government Citizenship

Culture

Fast Fact 100

Dancer and choreographer Twyla Tharp combines ballet, modern dance, and pop music in her programs.

Twyla Tharp is said to be an innovator. What is an *innovator*?

Fast Fact 101

A compass rose is a map symbol that shows the directions north, south, east, and west.

What state names include compass directions?

Geography

Fast Fact 102

In 1882 Peter J. McGuire, an early labor leader, suggested the idea of a Labor Day holiday to honor working people.

When is Labor Day celebrated?

Fast Fact 103

From 1969 to 2001, twenty-seven American economists have won the Nobel Prize in Economic Science.

What are the other five areas in which a person can win a Nobel Prize?

Economics

Fast Fact 104

The United States and twenty other countries from North, Central, and South America formed the Organization of American States to promote good relations among the countries of the Americas.

Are North, Central, and South America in the Eastern Hemisphere or the Western Hemisphere?

Fast Fact 105

The Korean day of thanksgiving, called Chusongnal, is in September. It celebrates the end of the rice harvest.

When is the United States thanksgiving holiday celebrated?

Culture

Geography

Fast Fact 106

Michigan is divided into two parts by a body of water.

Which of the Great Lakes is the only one that does not touch the state of Michigan?

Fast Fact 107

The Mason-Dixon line gets its name from the two English surveyors who determined this boundary line.

What two states' borders are determined by the Mason-Dixon line?

Economics

Fast Fact 108

Jack Kilby began the electronic age in 1958 by developing the idea of the silicon chip, which led to the development of semiconductors.

What electronic devices do you use at home and at school?

Fast Fact 109

John Hancock signed the bottom of the Declaration of Independence in huge letters so that the King of England could read it without his glasses!

When someone tells you to "put your John Hancock here," what do they mean?

Government Citizenship

Culture

Fast Fact 110

American painter Mary Cassatt was born in Pennsylvania, but she lived most of her adult life in France.

What other famous American artists do you know about? What did they like to show in their paintings, sculptures, or other works?

Fast Fact 111

The Spanish word *baja* means "below." Baja California is a peninsula that is part of the country of Mexico. It is just below California!

What state in the southeast of the United States is a peninsula?

Geography

Fast Fact 112

The cliff dwellings in Mesa Verde National Park are about 700 years old.

In what state is Mesa Verde National Park?

Fast Fact 113

Coupon comes from a French word meaning "to cut."

Why do people use coupons?

Economics

Government
Citizenship

Fast Fact 114

In ancient Rome candidates for office wore white clothes to show their spotless records.

What are some things people running for office in modern times do to get elected?

Fast Fact 115

George Ferris built the first Ferris wheel in 1893 for the World's Columbian Exposition in Chicago, Illinois.

Where can you ride on a Ferris wheel in the United States today?

Culture

Geography

Fast Fact 116

Christopher Columbus named the island where he landed San Juan Bautista. The port city on the island was called Puerto Rico. Now the city is called San Juan, and the island country is called Puerto Rico.

About how many miles is it from Key West, Florida, to San Juan, Puerto Rico?

Fast Fact 117

Explorer Ferdinand Magellan named the Pacific Ocean. *Pacific* means "peaceful," and Magellan's ships had peaceful weather on the Pacific Ocean.

What ocean borders the east coast of the United States?

History

Economics

Fast Fact 118

Thousands of miles of pipelines move oil and natural gas to locations all over the nation.

How would an extremely cold winter affect the demand for oil and natural gas?

Fast Fact 119

George Washington created the Purple Heart award in 1782 to be given to soldiers who demonstrated military bravery.

For what is the Purple Heart awarded to military people today?

Government Citizenship

Culture

Fast Fact 120

Texan Lance Armstrong won the Tour de France, a 2,150-mile bicycle race, four times in a row.

Where does the Tour de France take place? Find it on a map.

Fast Fact 121

The name *Alabama* came from Native American words meaning "I clear the thicket."

What states border the state of Alabama?

Geography

History

Fast Fact 122

Levi and Katie Coffin of Fountain City, Indiana, helped more than 2,000 slaves escape to Canada on the Underground Railroad.

What was the Fugitive Slave Act?

Fast Fact 123

Bankrupt comes from Italian words meaning "broken" and "bench." Long ago merchants did business in public on benches. When merchants could not pay their debts, their benches were said to be broken.

What does it mean today when someone says that he or she is "broke"?

Economics

Government
Citizenship

Fast Fact 124

John Burke was known as General Robert E. Lee's favorite spy. Burke used disguises to get through enemy lines.

Who was General Robert E. Lee?

Fast Fact 125

Horace Mann of Massachusetts, called the father of American public education, helped to establish the first state board of education in the country in 1837.

How many days long is the school year in your school district?

Culture

Geography

Fast Fact 126

Geyser comes from an Icelandic word meaning "to gush." A geyser is a spring that spouts a fountain of hot water and steam into the air at regular intervals.

What famous geyser can you see at Yellowstone National Park?

Fast Fact 127

Three pence per pound. That is the amount of the tax that the British levied on the colonists' tea, which was one the causes of the Boston Tea Party in 1773.

Into what body of water did the colonists dump the tea?

History

Economics

Fast Fact 128

Calculate **comes from a Latin word meaning "pebble." Long ago people used piles of stones to do arithmetic.**

What do people use today to figure out mathematical problems?

Fast Fact 131

The Platte River in Nebraska is named for a French word meaning "flat." The Platte is a smooth, slow-moving river.

Where in Nebraska is the Platte River?

Geography

History

Fast Fact 132

The Creek people were forced to move from Alabama to Oklahoma. They named their new settlement Tulsa, which was also the name of their old home in Alabama.

Many settlers named new places after the places they came from. How many state names have the word *New* in them? What are they?

Fast Fact 133

Spanish doubloons were coins worth twice as much as certain other coins.

What coins do we use today that are worth twice as much as another coin?

Economics

Fast Fact 134

United States interstate highways that go north-south are numbered with sequential odd numbers starting in the West. East-west interstates are numbered with sequential even numbers starting in the South.

What is the closest north-south interstate near your home? the closest east-west interstate?

Fast Fact 135

New Hampshire license plates, which are manufactured by prisoners in the state prison in Concord, bear the slogan "Live Free or Die."

What slogan or motto appears on the license plates of your state?

Culture

Fast Fact 136

The Rocky Mountains were named after a Native American tribe, the Assiniboin. *Assiniboin* means "rocks."

Where in North America are the Rocky Mountains?

Fast Fact 129

Veto comes from a Latin word meaning "I forbid." Today *veto* means "the right to reject a bill passed by a lawmaking group."

Who in the federal government has veto power? in state government?

Culture

Fast Fact 130

Benjamin Franklin's annual publication, *Poor Richard's Almanack*, contained proverbs, or words of advice, such as "A penny saved is a penny earned."

What proverbs have you heard or read?

Fast Fact 137

It was against the law in the South before the Civil War for a slave to learn to read and write.

Who was Frederick Douglass?

History

Economics

Fast Fact 138

A shopkeeper buys goods at wholesale and sells them at retail. The wholesale price of a pair of shoes might be $20, and the retail price might be $35.

What retail stores do you know of in your community, and what do they sell?

Fast Fact 139

Dedicated in 1996, the Grand Staircase-Escalante National Monument in southern Utah is three times the size of Rhode Island.

How does Rhode Island compare in size to the other states?

Government Citizenship

Fast Fact 140

The "Lindy" was a popular dance in the 1940s. It was named after aviator Charles Lindbergh.

What are some other dances that have been popular in the past?

Government Citizenship

Fast Fact 144

Oops! The U.S. Postal Service issued a Grand Canyon stamp in January of 2000 with the image reversed! It was too expensive to reprint the stamps, so they were released like that.

How much does it cost to send a first-class letter by U.S. mail?

Fast Fact 143

About 85 percent of all families in the United States own one car, and about 35 percent own two or more.

How might people who do not own a car move around a city?

Economics

Fast Fact 145

Queen Liliuokalani was queen of the Hawaiian Islands from 1891–1893.

What are the names of the six largest Hawaiian Islands?

Culture

Fast Fact 146

Whooping cranes, an endangered species, migrate from northwestern Alberta, Canada, to the Aransas National Wildlife Refuge in Texas every fall.

About how many miles is it from the northwest corner of Alberta to Aransas Pass, Texas?

Fast Fact 147

Legend says that Betsy Ross of Philadelphia, Pennsylvania, sewed the first red, white, and blue flag of the United States of America.

What historical sights can you see if you visit Philadelphia, Pennsylvania?

History

Economics

Fast Fact 148

Goobers! The United States grows about 10 percent of the world's peanut crop.

In which region of the United States is most of the peanut crop grown?

Fast Fact 149

In 1956 President Dwight D. Eisenhower signed the Federal-Aid Highway Act, which created the Interstate Highway System.

What is the difference in meaning between the words *interstate* and *intrastate*?

Government Citizenship

Culture

Fast Fact 150

American author Mark Twain took his pen name from a Mississippi River phrase, *mark twain*, which means "two fathoms deep."

What was Mark Twain's real name?

Fast Fact 151

Atlanta, Georgia, was first called Terminus because it was the last stop of the Western and Atlantic Railroad. Then it was called Marthasville. It was named Atlanta in 1845.

In what region of the country is Atlanta, Georgia?

Geography

History

Fast Fact 152

When Virginia seceded from the Union in 1861, people in the western part of the state wanted to remain in the Union. West Virginia, originally called Kanawha, was admitted as a state in 1863.

What states border West Virginia?

Fast Fact 153

Pass the pancakes! Maple syrup is an important product made in Vermont.

How is maple syrup made?

Economics

Government Citizenship

Fast Fact 154

The city of Denver, Colorado, has the largest park system in the United States. There are 200 parks within the city limit.

How do cities pay for parks and park programs?

Fast Fact 141

Maine was once known as the "Earmuff Capital of the World" because they were invented there in 1873 by Chester Greenwood.

What is the climate of Maine like?

Geography

History

Fast Fact 142

The Lincoln Highway, the first paved highway to cross the United States, was completed in 1925.

About how many miles is it from New York to San Francisco, the beginning and ending cities of the Lincoln Highway?

Fast Fact 155

Before it became a patriotic song of the American Revolution, the song "Yankee Doodle" was an insult. *Yankee* was an insulting name for a New Englander, and *doodle* meant "a fool."

What other patriotic songs do you know?

Culture

Fast Fact 156

You need scuba gear to visit Monterey Canyon! It is an underwater canyon, about the size of the Grand Canyon, in Monterey Bay in California.

Where in California is Monterey Bay?

Fast Fact 157

"The summer soldier and the sunshine patriot will, in this crisis, shrink from the service of his country. . . ." wrote Thomas Paine during the Revolutionary War.

What does Paine mean by a "summer soldier" and a "sunshine patriot"?

History

Economics

Fast Fact 158

In 1914 the Ford Auto Company paid adult workers $5.00 per day, twice as much as workers in other car factories were being paid.

In what state did Henry Ford build his car factory?

Fast Fact 159

One of the first United States passports was issued in 1778.

Who needs a United States passport?

Government Citizenship

Culture

Fast Fact 160

Cleveland, Ohio, is home to the Rock and Roll Hall of Fame, which opened in 1995.

Who are your favorite rock and roll artists?

Fast Fact 161

The geographical center of the continental United States is near Lebanon, Kansas. The geographical center of North America is near Rugby, North Dakota.

What river runs through North Dakota and South Dakota, and forms the eastern border of Nebraska?

Geography

History

Fast Fact 162

Molly Pitcher, whose real name was Mary Ludwig Hays McCauley, got her nickname from carrying water to thirsty soldiers during a battle in the Revolutionary War.

What states border New Jersey, the site of the battle of Monmouth?

Fast Fact 163

The United States $10 bill pictures Alexander Hamilton, and the $100 bill pictures Benjamin Franklin. All other bills picture presidents.

What United States presidents are pictured on the $5 and $20 bills?

Economics

Fast Fact 164

The federal government owns about 32 percent of all of the land in the United States.

How do you think the federal government uses this land?

Fast Fact 165

New Jersey has a museum that displays a collection of more than 5,400 spoons from every state and almost every country.

What museums can you visit near your home? What do those museums collect?

Culture

Geography

Fast Fact 166

Frozen grasshoppers! Millions of grasshoppers are embedded in the ice of Grasshopper Glacier, which is in the Custer National Forest in Montana.

In what state is most of Yellowstone National Park, the first national park in the United States?

Fast Fact 167

The first permanent settlements in Kansas were forts—Fort Leavenworth, Fort Scott, and Fort Riley. They were built to protect travelers on the Santa Fe and Oregon Trails.

Where did the Santa Fe and Oregon Trails begin and end?

History

Economics

Fast Fact 168

Ronald Reagan, the 40th president of the United States, studied economics in college.

What jobs did Ronald Reagan hold before he became president?

Fast Fact 169

In ancient Rome, pebbles were used to cast votes for or against a law. A black pebble was a vote against a law. A white pebble was a vote for a law.

What branch of the U.S. government makes our laws?

Government Citizenship

Culture

Fast Fact 170

You might hear Polish being spoken on the streets of Chicago, Illinois, because it is home to the world's largest population of Poles outside of Warsaw, Poland.

What language or languages besides English are spoken in your community?

Fast Fact 171

Tornado Alley runs right through the Midwest. On April 3 and 4 of 1974, the Midwest was hit with 148 tornadoes. The damages cost more than 600 million dollars, and 315 people died.

What does a tornado look like?

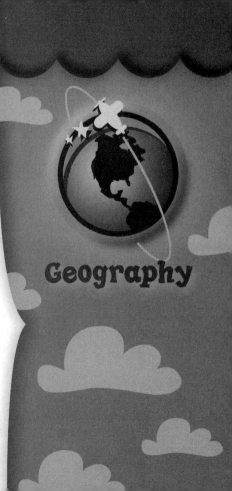

Geography

History

Fast Fact 172

President Franklin Delano Roosevelt was the first United States president to have a presidential aircraft. His plane was nicknamed *The Sacred Cow*.

During what years did Franklin Delano Roosevelt serve as president?

Fast Fact 173

Madam C.J. Walker, an African American woman who built a door-to-door cosmetic sales business, became one of the nation's first woman millionaires.

What is an entrepreneur?

Economics

Fast Fact 174

Barry Goldwater, who once ran for president, was born in Arizona before it became a state.

What are the requirements for someone to serve as president?

Fast Fact 175

Six presidents have been named James, or a variation of James: James Madison, James Monroe, James Polk, James Buchanan, James Garfield, and Jimmy Carter.

What is the most common girl's name in your classroom? boy's name?

Culture

Geography

Fast Fact 176

Mount Waialeale on the Hawaiian island of Kauai is the rainiest spot in the United States. It gets about 480 inches of rain each year.

What place in the United States gets the least amount of rain each year?

Fast Fact 177

Gerald Ford served as a vice-president and as a president of the United States, but he was not elected to either office.

How did Gerald Ford become vice-president and then president of the United States?

History

Economics

Fast Fact 178

The Golden Dollar Coin, which replaces the Susan B. Anthony coin, features Sacagawea and her infant son on one side.

Who did Sacagawea assist in their travels?

Fast Fact 179

The Pentagon is one of the biggest office buildings in the world. It has more than three million square feet of office space.

Who works in the Pentagon?

Government Citizenship

Culture

Fast Fact 180

Have you ever heard of Doghouse Junction, California; Toad Hop, Indiana; or Monkey's Eyebrow, Kentucky? These are all the names of real towns.

What are the most unusual town names in your state?

Fast Facts Answers

1. California, the West
2. George Washington, Thomas Jefferson, James Madison, James Monroe, William Henry Harrison, John Tyler, Zachary Taylor, Woodrow Wilson
3. Cattle used to roam freely on the plains. With the invention of barbed wire, smaller farmers could fence in their land and survive. Barbed wire ended the open range.
4. Abigail Adams and Barbara Bush
5. Answers will vary.
6. the West
7. Angel Island in the San Francisco Bay
8. A teller is a bank cashier who takes in and gives out money.
9. the judicial branch
10. sod
11. Death Valley
12. Spain
13. the United States government (the United States Mint and the Bureau of Engraving and Printing)
14. Federal Bureau of Investigation
15. Answers will vary.
16. the West
17. Wilbur and Orville Wright
18. Florida has a tropical climate. It is warm and wet.
19. Answers will vary.
20. New Mexico is in the Southwest. It has dry, flat regions as well as mountainous regions.
21. The Mississippi River begins in Minnesota and empties into the Gulf of Mexico in Louisiana.
22. Sequoyah
23. Shoppers might use a budget to know how much money they have, how much they need for expenses, how much they want to save, and how much they have to spend.
24. 18

25. Answers will vary but may include apple pie, ice cream cones, fried chicken, barbecued ribs, and so on.
26. the United States and Canada
27. Florida, the Southeast
28. an export
29. 100 senators, 435 representatives
30. Answers will vary.
31. the West
32. Washington, D.C.
33. George Washington
34. the vice-president
35. Answers will vary.
36. Maine, New Hampshire, Massachusetts, Rhode Island, Connecticut, New York, New Jersey, Delaware, Maryland, Virginia, North Carolina, South Carolina, Georgia, and Florida
37. Gerald Ford
38. to sell products or services
39. amendments
40. Answers will vary.
41. Alaska, Washington, Oregon, California, and Hawaii
42. 1861–1865
43. renewable
44. the executive branch
45. Answers will vary but may include Mount Rushmore and the Badlands.
46. Washington is in the northwest corner of the contiguous United States. It shares a border with Canada to its north. It is on the Pacific Ocean.
47. the Bill of Rights
48. The serial number appears twice on the front side of a bill.
49. Answers will vary depending on the political party of the incumbent president.
50. Answers will vary.
51. 6,000,000,000; nine zeros

52. Virginia, North Carolina, South Carolina, Georgia, Florida, Alabama, Tennessee, Mississippi, Louisiana, Arkansas, and Texas
53. Washington
54. John Adams, Thomas Jefferson, Martin Van Buren, Theodore Roosevelt, Calvin Coolidge, Harry S. Truman, Lyndon Baines Johnson, Richard M. Nixon, and George H. W. Bush
55. radio, television, movies, Internet, telephone
56. Arizona, Utah, Colorado, Oklahoma, and Texas
57. petroleum, timber, minerals, fish
58. If transportation costs are high, the price of the goods will also be high.
59. every four years
60. Answers will vary.
61. Lake Huron, Lake Erie, Lake Ontario, Lake Michigan, and Lake Superior; they begin in the Northeast region and end in the Midwest.
62. The Louisiana Purchase extended from the Mississippi River to the Rocky Mountains and from Canada to the Gulf of Mexico.
63. Both wages and salary are payment for work done. Wages are hourly compensation; a salary is a fixed amount of money that a worker gets for a specified period of time, such as a week or a month.
64. The Secret Service protects the president and vice-president and their families.
65. Answers may include the White House, Congress, the Washington Monument, and so on.
66. Minnesota, Wisconsin, Iowa, Illinois, Missouri, Kentucky, Tennessee, Arkansas, Mississippi, and Louisiana
67. Answers will vary.
68. The bald eagle is one of the symbols of our country.
69. George Washington
70. Answers may include that Indianapolis is the capital of Indiana.
71. New Hampshire, Vermont, New York, Connecticut, and Rhode Island

72. Queen Isabella funded Columbus's voyages to the Americas.
73. a small part of a company or corporation
74. Answers will vary.
75. Answers will vary.
76. Answers will vary.
77. A suffragette worked to help women get the right to vote.
78. A boycott is an agreement not to buy a product in order to force a change in the supplier's policy. A strike is a work stoppage by employees to get better pay, better hours, or some other benefit.
79. Austin
80. Answers will vary but may include words such as *taco, chili, frijoles, rodeo,* and so on.
81. Hawaii is made up entirely of islands.
82. Citizens of the Texas territory were fighting against Santa Anna and the Mexican Army. The Mexican Army won the Battle of the Alamo.
83. Gold is valuable, and so is oil.
84. A capital is a city; a capitol is a building.
85. Mexico's victory over French invaders in 1862
86. Utah, Colorado, New Mexico, and Arizona
87. Abraham Lincoln
88. The United States was in the middle of the Great Depression and few people were buying new cars.
89. a Texan who was the 36th president of the United States
90. Students should be able to point out Haiti and South Carolina on a map.
91. Asia
92. Mexico
93. The price of beaver hats would probably go down as the supply of beaver fur increased.
94. "Old Glory" or "Stars and Stripes"
95. Thanksgiving
96. the Gulf of Mexico
97. Answers will vary.
98. raising cattle
99. Governor of Texas
100. An innovator is someone who tries new ways of doing things.

101. North Carolina, North Dakota, South Carolina, South Dakota, West Virginia
102. the first Monday in September
103. physics, chemistry, medicine or physiology, literature, the promoting of peace
104. the Western Hemisphere
105. the fourth Thursday in November
106. Lake Ontario
107. Pennsylvania and Maryland
108. Answers may include computers, handheld computers, DVDs, and so on.
109. to sign your name
110. Answers will vary.
111. Florida
112. Colorado
113. to save money on a product or at a certain store
114. give speeches, advertise on radio and television, hang posters, give out campaign literature
115. at carnivals or amusement parks
116. about 1,100 miles
117. the Atlantic Ocean
118. The demand for fuel to heat homes and places of business would increase.
119. for being wounded or killed by enemy forces
120. France
121. Mississippi, Tennessee, Georgia, and Florida
122. a federal law that required citizens of all states to help capture escaped slaves
123. The person has no money.
124. an important general in the Confederate Army
125. Answers will vary.
126. Old Faithful
127. Boston Harbor
128. paper and pencils, adding machines, calculators, computers
129. the president; the governor
130. Answers will vary.
131. It runs east-west in the southern part of the state.
132. four; New Hampshire, New Jersey, New

Mexico, and New York

133. A dime is worth two nickels, a fifty-cent piece is worth two quarters, and a dollar coin is worth two fifty-cent pieces.
134. Answers will vary.
135. Answers will vary.
136. They are in the West and run from Canada to New Mexico.
137. He was an African American man who escaped from slavery and wrote a book called *A Narrative of the Life of Frederick Douglass*.
138. Answers will vary.
139. It is the smallest state.
140. Answers may include the waltz, Charleston, jitterbug, twist, break dancing, and so on.
141. Maine is temperate in the summer and cold and snowy in the winter.
142. about 2,600 miles
143. by walking or by public transportation, such as train, bus, or taxi

144. 37 cents as of 2002
145. Hawaii, Maui, Lanai, Molokai, Oahu, and Kauai
146. about 2,400 miles
147. Answers may include Betsy Ross's house, the Liberty Bell, and Independence Hall.
148. the Southeast
149. *Interstate* means between states; *intrastate* means within a state.
150. Samuel Langhorne Clemens
151. the Southeast
152. Kentucky, Ohio, Pennsylvania, Maryland, and Virginia
153. Sugar maple trees are tapped in early spring, and the sap is collected in buckets. The sap is boiled down to make maple syrup.
154. with taxes and fees
155. Answers will vary but may include "America, the Beautiful" or "The Star-Spangled Banner."
156. Monterey Bay is near the center of coastal California.

157. Paine suggests that these kinds of soldiers and patriots will not be loyal to the country when times get tough.
158. Michigan
159. a United States citizen traveling to another country
160. Answers will vary.
161. the Missouri River
162. Delaware, Pennsylvania, and New York
163. Abraham Lincoln and Andrew Jackson
164. Answers may include land for federal office buildings, land for national parks, and land for roads.
165. Answers will vary.
166. Wyoming
167. The Santa Fe Trail began at Independence, Missouri, and ended in Santa Fe, New Mexico. The Oregon Trail began at Independence, Missouri, and ended in Oregon City, Oregon.
168. He was a radio sportscaster, an actor, and a governor of California.
169. the legislative branch
170. Answers will vary.
171. A tornado extends down from a mass of dark clouds and looks like a twisting funnel.
172. 1933–1945
173. a person who organizes and manages a business
174. A person must be born in the United States, be at least 35 years old, and be a resident of the United States for at least 14 years.
175. Answers will vary.
176. Death Valley, California
177. Gerald Ford was appointed as vice-president by President Nixon after Spiro Agnew resigned the office. When President Nixon resigned because of the Watergate scandal, Ford succeeded him as president.
178. the Lewis and Clark Expedition
179. people who work for the Department of Defense
180. Answers will vary.